Important
UNITED STATES
Moments

September 11, 2001

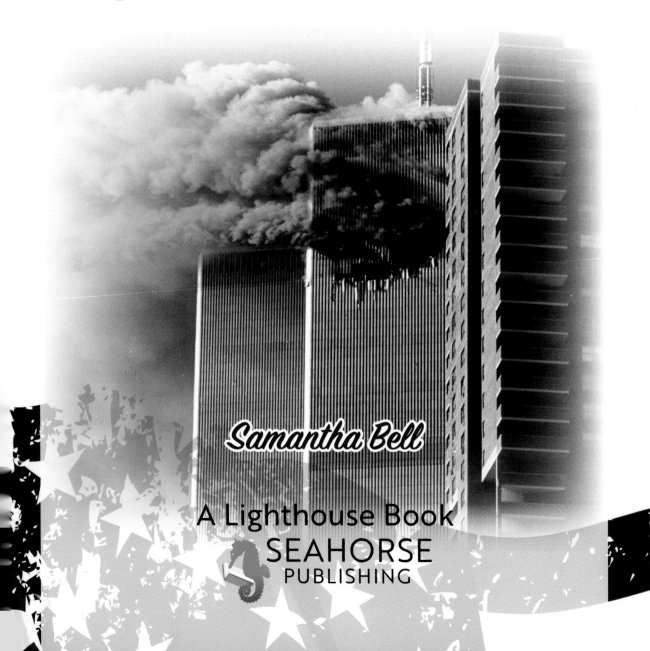

Samantha Bell

A Lighthouse Book
SEAHORSE
PUBLISHING

Teaching Tips for Caregivers:

As a caregiver, you can help your child succeed in school by giving them a strong foundation in language and literacy skills and a desire to learn by reading.

Reading for pleasure and interest will help your child to develop reading skills and will provide the opportunity to practice these skills in meaningful ways. Use the following strategies.

- Encourage the student to read independently at home.
- Encourage the student to practice reading aloud.
- Encourage activities that require reading.
- Establish a regular reading time.
- Have the student write questions about what they read.

Teaching Tips for Teachers:

Engage students throughout the reading process by asking questions. Sample responses are provided.

Before Reading:

- What do I know about the date September 11, 2001?
  I know terrorists hijacked American airplanes.
  I know the Twin Towers in New York City collapsed.

- What do I want to learn about September 11th?
  I want to learn what happened on that day.
  I want to learn why the towers fell.

During Reading:

- I am curious to know...
  I am curious to know how many planes were hijacked.
  I am curious to know what happened to the terrorists.

- How is this like something I already know?
  We talk about September 11th in my class at school every year.
  I have seen the American flag lowered to half-mast on September 11th.

After Reading:

- What was the author trying to teach me?
  The author was trying to teach me about the deadly actions of the terrorists and the heroic actions of individual Americans.
  The author was trying to teach me that Americans became united in their feelings of sadness and patriotism.

- How did the pictures and captions help me understand more?
  The graphic of the Twin Towers helped me understand where the buildings were hit.
  The photo of people covered in dust from the collapsed towers gave me an idea of what they went through that day.

TABLE OF CONTENTS

Chapter 1

Hijacked!

Al-Qaeda is one of the most powerful **terrorist** groups in the world. Terrorists are people who use **intimidation** or violence to make people afraid. They usually do it for political reasons.

On September 11, 2001, members of al-Qaeda **hijacked** four airplanes full of passengers. They flew the planes toward important places in the United States. They planned to use the planes as weapons to damage buildings and hurt people.

Osama bin Laden

MEMORY BANK

The founder of al-Qaeda was Osama bin Laden. Under his leadership, al-Qaeda launched attacks and bombings in many nations. In 2001, his group was based in the country of Afghanistan.

United States

Afghanistan

Two of the planes headed to New York City. They targeted the Twin Towers, the tallest buildings in the city. The towers were part of the World Trade Center where many bankers and other influential people worked.

The third plane flew to Arlington, Virginia. It hit the Pentagon. This important building is the **headquarters** of the U.S. Department of Defense. It is also the headquarters of the U.S. Army, Navy, and Air Force.

The Twin Towers

The Pentagon

The fourth plane did not hit its target. It crashed in a field near Shanksville, Pennsylvania.

Almost 3,000 people were killed in the attacks. This terrible day became known as 9/11.

Shanksville Field

New York City

Shanksville •

Arlington

Chapter 2

The Twin Towers

The World Trade Center was a large complex in New York City. It included seven buildings, a large plaza, and an underground shopping mall. The Twin Towers stood at the center of the complex. Each tower had 110 floors.

On the morning of September 11, 2001, both towers were full of people working in offices and following their daily routines.

At 8:46 a.m. Eastern Standard Time, the first plane crashed into the North Tower near the 95th floor.

The plane hit the tower with tremendous force. The jet fuel **ignited**. The tower was left with a giant, burning hole. Hundreds of people were killed instantly.

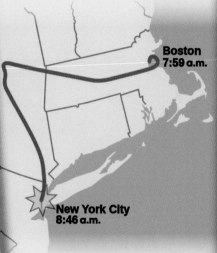

People were trapped in the North Tower on the floors above the crash site. People below the site started to **evacuate**. Many people thought there had been some kind of accident.

Then, at 9:03 a.m., the second plane hit the South Tower. It crashed near the 80th floor. Hundreds more people were killed on impact. It was clear the United States was under attack.

North Tower Impact on 93rd-99th floors

South Tower Impact on 77th-85th floors

MEMORY BANK

The first plane to crash was American Airlines Flight 11. It had 76 passengers and 11 crew members. The second plane was United Airlines Flight 175. It carried 51 passengers and nine crew members. There were five hijackers on each flight.

Boston
8:15 a.m.

New York City
9:03 a.m.

United Airlines Flight 175 took this route before it crashed into the South Tower.

Chapter 3

The Pentagon

Millions of people were watching the events in New York City on television. But the attack was not over yet. At 9:37 a.m., the third plane crashed into the Pentagon.

The aircraft flew into the west wall of the building's first floor. All 64 people onboard died when it hit. The crash also set off a chain of events that damaged the building and killed 125 people inside. Most were Army and Navy service members.

American Airlines Flight 77 took off from Washington, D.C., at 8:20 a.m. It was bound for Los Angeles, California. The plane took this route before it hit the Pentagon.

The Pentagon is only about two miles (three kilometers) from the White House in Washington, D.C. People feared that there would be more attacks on the nation's capital city and leaders.

On that day, President George W. Bush was visiting a school in Florida. But Vice President Dick Cheney was in the White House. Secret Service agents evacuated the Vice President and his aides. They went to a **bunker** beneath the White House.

President Bush was reading to elementary school students that morning. When he was told about the North Tower, he thought it must be an accident.

Chapter 4

The Towers Collapse

The Twin Towers were built in 1973. They were designed to withstand many things. In the past, they had stood up against hurricane-force winds.

But the towers could not survive the fires that raged through them after the plane crashes. The high temperatures weakened the steel that supported them.

President Bush talked to first responders at the crash sites.

President Bush made a speech to the American people. He said, "Terrorist attacks can shake the foundations of our biggest buildings, but they cannot touch the foundation of America. These acts shatter steel, but they cannot dent the steel of American resolve."

17

At 9:59 a.m., about an hour after the second crash, the South Tower collapsed. The upper floors fell on the lower ones until the whole **structure** came down. About 30 minutes later, the North Tower fell in the same way.

Massive clouds of dust and smoke poured through the city streets. The entire World Trade Center complex was destroyed.

The South Tower burned for 56 minutes. It collapsed in 10 seconds.

Only 20 people in the towers survived the collapse. More than 2,000 people died. Thousands more were treated for injuries.

The North Tower burned for 102 minutes before its collapse.

MEMORY BANK

New York City firefighters were the first responders who went into the buildings to rescue the people trapped inside. A total of 343 firefighters lost their lives trying to save others.

A New York City firefighter calls for the help of 10 more rescue workers.

Chapter 5

Flight 93

The fourth plane left from New Jersey for a flight to San Francisco, California. It was delayed on the runway. It took off just minutes before the first plane hit the North Tower.

At 9:24 a.m., the pilot got a radio warning. It said that planes had crashed at the World Trade Center. It told the pilot to be on alert. There was not much time to respond. At 9:28 a.m., Flight 93 was hijacked.

Newark, New Jersey
8:42 a.m.

Shanksville, Pennsylvania
10:03 a.m.

United Airlines Flight 93 took this route before it crashed.

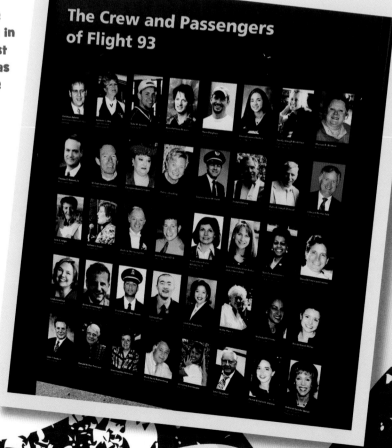

Passengers on Flight 93 used mobile phones to call family members and others. They got the news about what happened at the World Trade Center and the Pentagon. The passengers and flight attendants took a vote. They decided to fight.

Passenger Todd Beamer called a phone operator. He talked about joining others in a plan to fight back against the hijackers. The group was almost ready to act. At the end of the call, Todd said, "Let's roll." Minutes later, the plane crashed.

The Crew and Passengers of Flight 93

Some passengers and crew members made a plan to keep the plane from reaching its target. They fought back against the four hijackers. Officials think they used a fire extinguisher to break into the plane's **cockpit** and attack the hijackers.

The plane crashed in a field near Shanksville, Pennsylvania. All 44 people aboard were killed.

The brave passengers and crew members kept Flight 93 from hitting its target and hurting more people. The plane was probably heading to the White House or the U.S. Capitol in Washington, D.C.

The White House

The Capitol Building

Flight 93 crashed in this field in Somerset County, Pennsylvania.

MEMORY BANK

You can visit the Flight 93 National Memorial in Pennsylvania near the field where the plane crashed. The Wall of Names there includes the name of each one of the 40 passengers and crew members on the flight. There is also a Tower of Voices. It has 40 wind-activated chimes to honor the voice of each person.

A common field one day. A field of honor forever.

A lookout lets visitors view the field.

Tower of Voices

Chapter 6

Never Forget

The tragic events of 9/11 brought the country together. Americans everywhere felt sadness. They shared a sense of grief.

Many people also felt **patriotic** and proud of their country. But the terrorist attacks made some people more fearful and suspicious.

MEMORY BANK

On September 11, 2011, a memorial opened in New York City. It was created to honor those killed on 9/11. It includes two reflecting pools with waterfalls. The waterfalls rush down where the Twin Towers used to stand. The names of 2,983 victims of terrorism are engraved on bronze panels surrounding the pools.

After September 11, 2001, the Global War on Terrorism began. This was an American-led military campaign against terrorists. It involved many different nations.

One of the first missions was Operation Enduring Freedom. It began on October 7, 2001. Within two months, U.S. forces had removed the Taliban from power. This was a terrorist group supported by al-Qaeda and Osama bin Laden.

Osama bin Laden himself was finally tracked down on May 2, 2011. He was killed by U.S. soldiers in the country of Pakistan.

For more than 10 years, the FBI and other U.S. intelligence and military agencies were on the hunt for Osama bin Laden.

Navy SEALs carried out the raid that killed Osama bin Laden.

In 2002, a new part of the U.S. government was created. It is the Department of Homeland Security (DHS). Its job is to detect and prevent terrorist activities in the U.S.

Some terrorist threats come from groups in other countries, like al-Qaeda or the Taliban. But some come from people in the United States. DHS tries to protect people from all types of terrorist attacks.

Each year on September 11th, Americans remember the terrible events of 9/11. They say, "We will never forget." They honor the victims of the attacks and promise to work toward a safer and more peaceful world.

9/11
PATRIOT DAY
★ ★ ★
WE WILL NEVER FORGET

American Airlines Flight 11
United Airlines Flight 175
American Airlines Flight 77
United Airlines Flight 93

Glossary

bunker (BUHNG-kur): an underground shelter, used especially during wartime

cockpit (KAHK-pit): the control area in the front of an airplane; the area from which the pilot and copilot control the plane

evacuate (i-VAK-yoo-ate): to leave a dangerous place

headquarters (HED-kwor-turz): the main building or office of an organization

hijacked (hye-JAKD): taken over and controlled by force

ignited (ig-NITE-id): caught on fire

intimidation (in-tim-i-DAY-shuhn): the act of making others fearful through threats or shows of power

patriotic (pay-tree-AH-tik): having a strong sense of love and loyalty to one's country

structure (STRUHK-chur): something that has been built, such as a building

terrorist (TER-ur-ist): related to people who use threats and violence to frighten others, obtain power, or force a government to do something

Index

Comprehension Questions

1. How many planes were hijacked on September 11, 2001?
  a. 2
  b. 4
  c. 3

2. Why did the hijackers target the Pentagon?
  a. The President of the United States might be there.
  b. It is located close to the nation's capital.
  c. It is the headquarters for the U.S. military.

3. Why did passengers on Flight 93 fight the hijackers?
  a. They knew more people would die if the hijackers made it to their destination.
  b. They knew they could defeat the hijackers and land the plane.
  c. They thought they would be able to turn around and finish their flight.

4. True or False: The Twin Towers were rebuilt in the same location.

5. True or False: The tremendous heat from the fires caused the Twin Towers to collapse.

Answer Key: 1. b, 2. c, 3. a, 4. False, 5. True

About the Author

Samantha Bell lives in the foothills of the Blue Ridge Mountains with her family and too many cats. She has written more than 150 nonfiction books for young readers. She enjoys drawing and painting, visiting new places, and spending time outdoors. She also loves learning about American history and even studied it in college.

Written by: Samantha Bell
Design by: Jen Bowers
Series Development: James Earley
Editor: Kim Thompson

Photo credits: cover: image ©2010 Ken Tannenbaum/Shutterstock, logo © Oleg latsun/ Shutterstock, clock border ©2012 liseykina/Shutterstock, flag border © nazlisart/Shutterstock; p.3, 29 ©2018 Brian E Kushner/Shutterstock; p.4 ©2019 muratart/Shutterstock; p.5 Public Domain/FBI.gov,© Volina/Shutterstock; p.6,11 ©2015 Joseph Sohm/Shutterstock; p.6 Public Domain/Department of Defense; p.7 ©2019 Rob Pauley/Shutterstock, © Ad_hominemShutterstock; p.8 ©2012 Joseph Sohm/Shutterstock; p.9 ©2010 Ken Tannenbaum/Shutterstock, Public Domain/ 9/11 commission; p.10 Public Domain/NIST/FOIA; p.11 Public Domain/ 9/11 commission; p.12 Public Domain/U.S. Navy Photo/Journalist 1st Class Mark D. Faram; p.13 Public Domain/U.S. Airforce Photo/Department of Defense; p.14 Public Domain/George W. Bush Presidential Library/National Archives; p.15 ©2010 Vacclav/Shutterstock; p.16 Public Domain/National Archives/add.archives.gov; p.17 Public Domain/George W. Bush Presidential Library/National Archives, ©2016 Sergey Uryadnikov/Shutterstock, ©2010 Susan Montgomery/Shutterstock; p.18 Public Domain/Pauljoffe, Public Domain/NIST/FOIA; p.19 ©2008 Anthony Correia/Shutterstock, Public Domain/U.S. Navy/Journalist 1st Class Preston Keres; p.20 Public Domain/9/11 commission, CC BY-SA 3.0/MacMax; p.21 CC BY 2.0, ©2021 JenBowers; p.22 ©2013 Andrea Izzotti/Shutterstock, ©2012 Orhan Cam/Shutterstock; p.23 Public Domain/U.S.Government, ©2021 Jen Bowers; p.24 ©2014 Rawpixel.com/Shutterstock; p.25 ©2017 James Carton/Shutterstock, ©2019 Reuber Duarte/Shutterstock; p.26 ©2021 Skorzewiak/Shutterstock; p.27 Public Domain/CIA, Public Domain/FBI, Public Domain/U.S. Air Force/Force Technical Sergeant Brian Snyder; p.28 Public Domain/Department of Homeland Security; p.29 © Greens87/Shutterstock, © kozer/Shutterstock

Library of Congress PCN Data
September 11, 2001 / Samantha Bell
Important United States Moments
ISBN 979-8-8873-5929-8 (hard cover)
ISBN 979-8-8873-5968-7 (paperback)
ISBN 979-8-8904-2027-5 (EPUB)
ISBN 979-8-8904-2086-2 (eBook)
Library of Congress Control Number: 2023912463

Printed in the United States of America.

Seahorse Publishing Company

www.seahorsepub.com

Published in the United States
Seahorse Publishing
PO Box 771325
Coral Springs, FL 33077